Raylene Uoth

Dairy Queen ®

Remember simpler times, when life moved at a slower pace? Having an ice cream or a float with friends and family was special; as much for the quality time spent together as the treats you shared. Well, life today seems to move at a much faster pace. But, the things that were important then are still important now. Like sharing, caring, and giving.

Dairy Queen believes in those traditional values. That's why we've supported the Children's Miracle Network since its inception 14 years ago. Dairy Queen stores in North America have raised over 50 million dollars in that time. This money has been used to update equipment, facilities and improve the quality of care at local Children's Hospitals.

And now, Dairy Queen is very excited to bring quality books to their patrons in the DQ Pick Nic Meal.

Dairy Queen knows the importance of reading. Being able to read is very important for making it through school, getting a good job and living daily life. It can be great entertainment, too, as you are swept away to another world through a great story.

One of the best ways to improve reading is by doing more of it. And, it's much easier to be excited about reading, if you enjoy the story! We're sure you are going to love the stories we are bringing to you in our Pick Nic Meals! These high-quality books reach a range of ages with adventure, action, and humor.

Maybe times haven't changed that much. Here at Dairy Queen, we still believe in old-fashioned values. The Dairy Queen System is very proud to have the opportunity to team up with the authors and publishers of these great books to help literacy across Canada.

W9-BIN-135

McCain Foods (Canada)
is a proud supplier to the
Canadian Dairy Queen System
and strongly supports the
***Dairy Queen Literacy
for Youth Program.***

If you're enjoying this book and looking for others in the series or others like it, they're available in bookstores everywhere. For a list of stores in your area where you can get these great books, go to:

www.coolreading.com

FICTION
SHORT cuts
SERIES ™

SNOWBOARDING...
TO THE EXTREME:
RIPPIN'

SIGMUND BROUWER

RIPPIN'

Published by coolreading.com, Red Deer, Alberta, Canada

Managing Editor: Mike Kooman.

Canadian Cataloguing in Publication Data

Brouwer, Sigmund, 1959–
    Rippin'

(Short cuts series)
ISBN 1-55305-011-8

I. Title. II. Series: Brouwer, Sigmund, 1959–
Short cuts series.

PS8553.R68467H57 2000   jC813'.54   C00-910110-1
PZ7.B79984Hi 2000

Printed in Canada

To
McKenna Breanne,
welcome to the clan.

Rippin' Glossary

For readers new to snowboarding, the following definitions may be helpful.

Boardhead	someone who loves snowboarding.
Fakie	riding the snowboard backwards.
Goofy	a person who snowboards with his right foot forward instead of his left foot forward.
Mogul	massive mounds on the ski hill.
Ollies	getting the snowboard into the air without using a jump.
Regular	a person who snowboards with his left foot forward.
Rippin'	snowboarding!
Surfing	snowboarding!
Wheelies	just like on a bike—snowboarding with the front end in the air.
Full spins	also known as a '360 Air'—jumping into the air and turning a full circle before landing.

Wipeout	a fall!
Nose bonk	hitting an object with the front of your snowboard.
Indy Poke	a move where the snowboarder grabs the toe edge of the board with the back hand while jumping.
Killer loops	great moves up and down the walls of the halfpipe.
Halfpipe	a giant groove in the hill, like a pipe cut in half, which snowboarders ride up and down the walls of the groove.
5-40s	the '540 Air' is a spin and a half, where the rider spins completely, then adds a half turn so that he or she ends up facing backward when landing.

Note to the reader: Different riders in different regions often come up with different names for the same tricks.

One

I stood at the top of the ski run. A mile below me was the finish line. Steve, my coach, waited beside me. He wanted me to reach that finish line in less time than it takes to eat a sandwich.

"Keegan," he said. "I can see that look on your face."

"What look?"

"You're thinking about Garth. Don't."

"Quit worrying about the speed, Keegan. Relax."

Of course, that's all I could think of.

SPEED. When I reach full speed, my skis will be moving at seventy miles per hour.

And I will be standing on those skis. I, too, will be moving seventy miles an hour. Almost as fast as people fall from airplanes before they open their parachutes.

I didn't have a parachute. Worse, skis are only about as wide as credit cards. My job is to stand on those narrow pieces of plastic and metal and make sure I don't fall at seventy miles per hour.

What I really don't like to think about is that, at seventy miles per hour, I'll be going 102 feet every second. My friend Joey, who likes to scare me, figured that out. Worse, after figuring it out, he told me. So now I know that in the time it takes for me to breathe in and out, my body will shoot the length of a football field.

At that speed, if I fall, I will spend the rest of my life in a hospital. Eating Jell-O. Drinking warm milk. Being bossed around by big, ugly nurses.

"Keegan, I still see that look on your face."

"Sorry," I said. I smiled, like I was actually going to enjoy this.

"That's better. Are you ready?" he asked.

"Sure," I answered. I wasn't going to let anyone know I was afraid. Not Keegan Bishop, state champion downhill skier.

"Now remember, when you get to the bottom, remind the timekeeper that you're wearing the wrong number."

I had on a small jersey with a big white number over my jacket. Another guy on the team, Budgie McGee, had accidentally taken my number. We didn't notice until he had started his trial. So I had his number on my back. It didn't matter, though, as long as I told the guys with the clipboards at the bottom of the hill.

I glanced at the timekeeper beside me. He nodded. I crouched and got ready.

"Go!" my coach yelled.

I went.

I blinked twice. The wind filled my lungs. It filled my ears like the roar of a freight train.

I cut left to miss an ice patch. I hit a jump at freeway speed. I flew into the air at least one story off the ground. I leaned forward and made sure my skis stayed straight.

I thumped back to earth and began to crouch to block less wind. At this speed, the trees on the sides of the run flashed by like fence boards.

Halfway down I knew I was skiing the best I ever had. If I kept pushing, I would easily stay number one.

Beneath my helmet, I grinned.

And as I cut into a steep turn, I saw it. But I couldn't believe it.

Wire. Black cable wire. Stretched between two trees. Waist high. With me screaming toward it at 102 feet per second. Hitting the wire at that speed would cut me in two.

TWO

I dropped my poles and sat on my skis. Balancing at seventy miles per hour on two thin pieces of plastic and metal, this was not as easy as sitting down for dinner. But I had no choice.

The wire scraped the top of my helmet as I slid beneath it. I wobbled. To keep my balance, I slapped my hand on the snow. My hand bounced off. The force nearly knocked me over the other way. I fought to stay on my skis for another hundred yards.

Finally, I was able to turn and dig the edges of my skis into the snow. I began to slow down.

But just when I thought I was safe, I hit a patch of ice. My skis slid out from under me. I began to tumble and roll down the hill. The sky tilted around me. The snow seemed to spin. The trees rose and fell at crazy angles. I felt like a cannonball bouncing down a set of stairs. Both of my skis popped loose as I rolled down the hill.

The best thing to do in a fall is also the hardest thing to do. You have to go limp like a rag doll. If you stay tight, you can rip your muscles and snap your bones.

I waited to stop tumbling. I finally fell into some deep, soft snow at the edge of the trees. I came to a stop with a whump!

I tasted for blood. Sometimes when you fall you bite your tongue. No blood.

I blinked. At least my eyelids worked.

I wiggled my fingers. They worked too.

So did my arms. And my legs.

That was a good sign. If I could move all my body parts, I knew I hadn't broken my back.

I thought about Garth. His accident happened two weeks ago. He was still in a hospital. Eating Jell-O. Drinking warm milk. Being bossed around by big, ugly nurses.

I took off my helmet and shook my hair loose.

Then I had another thought I didn't want to think. Black wire stretched between two trees is not an accident. What if the same thing had happened to Garth?

If Garth's broken legs weren't an accident, there were other questions I didn't want to ask.

Who was doing this? And why?

Three

I had my questions. But I also had something else to worry about.

That wire was still stretched between the trees. This run was closed for the racers to take timed practice runs. I was the last racer today. So I didn't have to worry about anyone else on our team. But now that I was finished, the run would be open to other skiers.

Any minute now, someone else might come over the hill. A kid, maybe. An old man or a woman. Someone who wouldn't be good enough to duck in time. A wire like that could kill someone!

I began to run back up the hill. It was not easy. I had to stay on hard-packed snow. Even then, my boots kept sinking in the snow. I felt like I was in one of those dreams where the monster is chasing you. No matter how hard you try to run, your shoes seem to be glued to the ground. I grabbed my skis as I passed them, but I didn't stop.

I kept running and looking up the hill to watch for skiers. I was ready to yell a warning if I saw someone.

I made it to the wire. No skiers yet. My heart was ready to explode. Running uphill in snow with ski boots on is hard work.

I saw that one end of the wire was wrapped around a tree trunk and twisted tight. It would have been easier to get it loose if I had pliers. But all I had were fingers and fear.

I began to untwist. The wire was heavy and stiff. It cut through my ski gloves. I kept untwisting. It cut into the skin of my fingers.

Finally, I had it nearly unwrapped.

I heard the swish of skis on snow.

Someone was coming down the hill!

All I saw was the shiny purple of a ski suit and flying blond hair. A girl came over the top of the rise and headed straight toward the wire! Not on skis, but on a snowboard.

"Stop!" I shouted. "Stop!"

Too late. She was going fast and didn't have a chance. The wire caught her across the middle of her body.

She screamed.

I thought the wire would slice her to pieces. It didn't.

I had untwisted just enough of the wire. She hit the wire hard and yanked the last bit of wire still around the tree loose. It flipped her over. As she fell, her snowboard and ankles got tangled in the wire. She slid for a bit. When she reached the end of the wire, it snapped her to a stop, just like when a dog runs to the end of its leash.

The girl yelped.

I ran over as fast as I could.

"Are you all right?" I asked as I helped her to her feet.

She didn't thank me for saving her life. She punched me in the face.

Four

"**H**ey!" I shouted. "What was that for?" "You jerk!" she shouted back. "You could have killed me!"

She took another swing at me. I grabbed her wrist just before her fist hit my face.

"Killed you?" I was breathing hard from running. My face hurt from her punch. And now this beautiful blond in a purple ski suit thought I had tried to kill her? "No way, I was trying to–"

"Do you think that kind of joke is funny?" She pulled her arm away from me. She gave me a dirty look. "What if you had tied the wire tight before I hit it? It could have sliced me in two."

"I was trying to untie it."

"Sure," she said. It didn't sound like she believed me though.

"The wire nearly got me too." I pointed down the hill. "I fell down there. I came back up the hill to untie it before anyone else got hurt."

I held out my hands so she could see the blood. "Here's where I cut my fingers. The wire is cold and hard to untwist."

"I'm sorry," she said. She looked at the ground. "You probably saved my life."

If this were a movie, she would have leaned forward and kissed me.

This wasn't a movie. I licked blood off my lip. It was dripping from my nose where she had punched me. Instead of kissing me, she unzipped a pocket and found some tissue. She wiped the blood off my face.

"What's your name?" she asked. Her accent was different. This ski hill was in Colorado. She sounded like the tourists who came from New York City.

"Keegan Bishop." I waited for her to say something about me being a great skier. Everyone who skied around here had heard of me.

"Keegan," she said. "I like that name. Are you a racer?"

I grinned. "You've heard of me?"

"No. I see the racing number on your back."

It was my turn to feel stupid. I tried to change the subject. "Are you from around here? Or are you on Christmas vacation?"

"My name's Cassie," she told me. "Cassie Holt. Thanks for asking."

Great. Now she probably thought I didn't even care what her name was. I should have asked her.

A couple of skiers passed us. They didn't say anything. Just kept on going.

I wondered when a ski official would show up to see why I hadn't made it to the bottom. I was going to wait right here. I wanted someone to see why I had fallen. That way, I would get a another chance to run my time trial.

It seemed like Cassie and I had stood there a long time without talking.

"Well," Cassie finally said, "if you didn't put the wire there, who did?"

"I'd like to know. Just so I could strangle them."

She smiled. "You're too cute to be that mean."

I didn't know what to say to that.

Cassie leaned down and popped the buckles of her bindings. She stepped out of her snow-board. She carried it under her arm and started to climb back up the hill. I stood there, staring at her purple ski suit and her long blond hair.

"Come on," she said.

"Where?"

"To the other tree."

"We can just pull the wire out of the way," I said. "We don't need to untie the other side." My hands hurt pretty bad. The coldness of the air did not help either.

Besides, I needed to be able to show the wire to my coach and the timekeepers. I wanted them to believe what happened.

"Who said anything about untying it?" she asked.

She walked to the other tree. She propped her snowboard against it and looked at the snow without moving. I finally walked up and stood beside her.

"Look at that," she said, pointing at marks in the snow.

"What?"

"Tracks. Whoever tied the wire to this tree stood right there."

"Maybe we should get a bloodhound," I said.

"Very funny, Keegan Bishop. Notice something about that track?"

"Belongs to a snowboard," I told her. It was a single wide track. From the marks in the snow, we could see where someone had walked around the tree as he tied the wire. We could see where someone had gotten on the snowboard and gone down a trail through the trees. No way to find him now.

"Snowboard," Cassie repeated. "So already you know something about the person who did this."

"That doesn't help much," I said. "There are only about a thousand people who snowboard here. Of course, not all of them are as good as this guy. He took a tough trail to escape. "

"He probably didn't want anyone to see him."

"And if no one saw him, we can't prove who did this."

"Not quite," she said. She pointed at a branch a little above my head. I saw some blue fuzz stuck to the branch. "The snowboarder who did this wears a blue knitted hat. It rubbed against that branch. So he must be as tall as you."

She put her hands on her hips and grinned at me. "A snowboarder. One with a blue hat. One who is tall. One who is good on a snowboard. There, now you know four things about the person who did this."

I grinned back. "What are you? A detective?"

Her grin turned into a frown. "I've got to go now."

"What did I say?" I asked.

She grabbed her snowboard and set it flat on the snow. She stepped into the bindings and tightened them.

"Cassie?" I tried again. "What did I say wrong?"

She didn't answer. She took off down the hill without looking back at me.

This girl had punched me in the face. She had wiped blood from my nose. She had insulted me. And she had left without saying goodbye.

This was some kind of girl.

I hoped I would meet her again soon.

Five

That night, I went to visit Garth in the hospital. He was in a room by himself in a big bed. His legs were in casts up to his waist. He wore pajama tops. There was a bowl of Jell-O on a tray in front of him. He didn't look happy.

"Keegan," he said. "This is a surprise."

It probably was. Garth Norwood is not exactly my friend. He is a little bigger than I am. And he's the kind of guy who tries to push people around. Right after I joined the ski team, he had tried it with me. We had nearly ended up in a fistfight.

"How are you?" he asked. He had long blond hair and a mustache.

"Almost not good," I said. "That's why I'm here. I nearly ended up in the hospital, too."

I explained to Garth what had happened with the wire.

"Really?" he said. "During time trials? Wow! That sounds terrible."

14

"It could have been worse," I said. "At least they're going to let me do another time trial. And Coach is going crazy about how I could have been hurt."

I looked at Garth and asked the question I had come for.

"What happened to you? All I know is that when the coach found you in the snow you were knocked out. And your legs were broken. You think maybe you could have hit a wire or something?"

"Nope," he said. "I crossed my ski tips. It's a stupid thing to do at the speed of a rocket."

"That's true," I said. "Very stupid."

"How's everyone else on the team? Has anything happened to anyone else?"

"No," I said. "Except for a minor jersey mix-up, nothing else has happened."

I told Garth about Budgie McGee, another skier on the team. He's the one who accidentally switched numbers with me before the time trials.

We both laughed at that. Budgie was Garth's best friend. Everyone calls him Budgie. His real name is Bud G. McGee. His tiny nose makes him kind of look like a budgie bird.

After laughing about Budgie, Garth and I couldn't find much to talk about. The same thing happens when we travel by bus to ski races. Garth and I don't much like being around each other.

"Well," I finally said, "time to go. I've got to get my homework done."

"Sure," he said.

I stood up. I got halfway to the door.

"Keegan."

I looked back at him.

"Yes?"

"Could you take this stupid meal tray?" he asked. "Maybe set it on the table over there?"

"No problem."

I walked back to his bed.

He picked up his tray and leaned forward to give it to me.

For a moment, his pajama top fell open. I was looking down at the tray, so I saw his chest and stomach.

I didn't say anything, though. I just set the tray on a table and said good-bye again.

As I walked down the shiny hallway of the hospital, I thought about Garth's stomach. I didn't like what I was thinking.

When his pajama top fell open, I saw that his entire stomach was black and blue. It looked like a giant bruise. It looked like the kind of bruise a wire cable would make if a skier hit it at full speed.

If Garth had hit a cable stretched between two trees, why had he lied to me about it?

Six

The next morning the sun was out again. The sky was bright blue, so pretty it almost hurt my eyes. There was no wind. And it was warmer than usual. It was a perfect day for skiing.

Except I wasn't thinking about skiing.

I got on the chairlift to the top of the mountain. As the chair moved, I hardly noticed the skiers and snowboarders going down the hill below me. All I could think about was that wire someone had tied between the trees yesterday.

Somebody had tried to hurt me bad.

I needed to find out who and why. If I didn't, that somebody might try again. The next time, though, I might not be so lucky. I was seventeen. I wanted to make it to my eighteenth birthday. And then many more until I was an old man. Running into cable wire at a high speed would not help my chances.

17

I needed to be a detective. But I knew a lot more about racing on skis than about looking for bad guys.

I grinned into the sunshine, thinking about something else. This would be more fun if the girl named Cassie Holt were helping me.

What had she said to me? The person who tied up the wire was tall. He wore a blue hat and could snowboard really well.

I guessed the first place I should look was where the snowboarders hung out. Which was where I was going. The best snowboarders liked a run that was called the Pipeline.

When I got off the chairlift, I skied over to that hill.

From the top, the run looked like a huge pipe with the top half cut off. There were trees on both sides of the run. Both sides of the run curved downward into the middle. It reminded me of the curved walls that skateboarders use to do their tricks.

I took my skis off and stuck them into the snow. Taking a seat on the ground, I watched the snowboarders. They did look like skateboarders as they went up and down the walls of the Pipeline. They did flips and turns. They did jumps and wipeouts*.

I heard a crunching of snow. I turned my head and looked upward. For a second, I couldn't see who was beside me. The sun was too bright.

"Hello, Keegan Bishop."

I knew the voice. It belonged to Cassie Holt.

"Hello," I said.

"Thinking of becoming a boardhead*?" she asked.

"Bored?" I asked. "No, actually I find this interesting. It looks a lot different from skiing."

She laughed. "I didn't ask if you found this boring. A boardhead is someone who snowboards."

"I knew that," I said. "I was just testing you."

"Right." She gave me a smile. "I've been asking people about you."

"Really?" My heart started to beat faster. Did this mean she'd been thinking about me like I'd been thinking about her?

"Really. They tell me that you live to be a downhill racer. I can understand why you don't know much about snowboarding."

"Well," I said. "I'm training as hard as I can to be a pro. It takes most of my time."

She nodded. "So why are you wasting time here?"

"I'm looking for a tall snowboarder with a blue hat," I told her. "Remember? Because of your..."

I stopped myself. If I said detective work, would she get mad again?

"Because of my detective work?" she asked. "Don't worry. I won't leave. Yesterday, I had a reason. Today I don't."

"What's the reason?"

"I can't tell you," she said. "Will you trust me on that?"

"Sure," I said.

Someone shouted at us.

"Hey, Cassie!" It was a guy on a snowboard, coming down from the top of the hill. The sun was in my eyes, so I couldn't see his face.

He stopped fast. He used the edge of his snowboard to throw snow all over me.

I stood up. The guy was a little taller than me. Although I didn't know his name, I had seen him before. He was one of the regular snowboarders.

"That's a jerk thing to do," I said. "Spraying snow like that."

"Sue me," he said. He looked at my skis stuck in the snow. "Think I'm scared of someone who doesn't have the guts to do some real surfing*?"

He spoke to Cassie. "Are you ready to go rippin'*?"

"Sure, Sid." Cassie smiled at me. "See you later, Keegan."

The two of them slid away on their snowboards.

The guy named Sid really carved the snow. He hit a jump and did a full spin around.

Cassie had just asked me to trust her.

So why was she snowboarding with a tall guy who was really good on a snowboard?

There was one other little thing that bothered me. One other little thing about this tall snowboarder that made it hard to trust Cassie.

He was wearing a blue knitted hat.

FICTION

SHORT cuts

SERIES™

Seven

I watched as they went down the hill. They didn't move nearly as fast as skiers. Instead, they looped up and down the slope.

Maybe I didn't like the guy with the blue hat simply because Cassie was with him. But it seemed to me that he loved to show off.

He hit a jump and spun a complete circle in the air. Off the next jump, he spun a circle and a half. He landed backward.

"Ooh," I heard someone say, "Did you see Sid hit that awesome 5-40*?"

They were moving farther and farther away. So I put my skis on to follow them.

Sid leaned way back on his snowboard. The nose of it tilted into the air. He grabbed it with one hand and rode the snowboard like someone doing a wheelie on a bicycle.

A little later, he hit another jump. He caught at least five feet of air. While still in the air, he kicked his heels upward. The snowboard was almost as high as his waist. He snagged the board with his closest hand and didn't let it go until just before landing.

"Check out that Indy Poke*!" someone called. "Sid's the best out here!"

I hoped he might fall, but he didn't. Instead he did trick after trick. Maybe he knew I was watching him. Maybe he knew I was grumpy about seeing him with Cassie.

Still, he was good, but I wouldn't admit that to anyone else. I wondered if he was good enough to have gotten away from the tree with the cable without being seen.

They reached the end of the run. I had no idea what to do next.

I wanted to keep following them. But I didn't want them to see me.

This was the Big Bear Ski Resort. I knew all of the runs at the resort. I knew all of the trails through the trees. I should. I have been skiing here since I was six years old.

The Pipeline ended where three other runs joined together. Then all four runs joined into one big run that ended at the main chairlift. I knew I could find them at the bottom. All I had to do was beat them there.

I grabbed my poles and pushed.

Downhill there was a break in the trees. I turned hard and ducked under some branches. It wasn't much of a trail, but to me, skiing is easier than running. I cut in and out of the trees at

23

nearly full speed. A few minutes later, I reached another ski run called the Roller Coaster.

I headed full out straight down the hill. I passed dozens of slower skiers. At the bottom of the hill, the Roller Coaster joined the Pipeline.

I slowed down and stopped in some trees at the side of the hill. The trees hid me from anyone coming down the Pipeline.

I waited.

A few minutes later, I saw Sid and Cassie. It was easy to see them. Sid had the blue hat and dark blue jacket. Cassie wore the purple ski suit. Both were carving major turns in the snow.

They hit the bottom and joined all the other skiers heading toward the chairlift.

I stayed back.

Two things helped me. One, people hardly ever look behind them when they are skiing or snowboarding. Two, there were a lot of skiers on this run. It would be hard to see me even if Sid or Cassie looked back.

But they didn't stop at the chairlift. They kept on going, right to the lodge where people buy lift tickets and change into their ski stuff. There's also a restaurant in there.

I thought it was strange. It was too early for lunch. Why were they ready to quit so soon?

I stayed back and kept watching.

Sid and Cassie stopped near the racks where people leave their equipment while they go inside. They stepped out of their snowboards and propped them against a rack. Then they walked into the building.

I skied over to a different set of racks. I kept watching them.

I felt stupid, though. What did I think I was going to learn by following them? I wasn't going to be able to get close enough to hear what they said.

This was my first try at being a detective, and already I felt like a loser.

Before I could decide what to do next, Sid and Cassie came back out of the building. They walked toward their snowboards.

I thought that was strange too. Why had they gone into the building and then come right out again?

I turned my head away so they could not see my face. When I looked back, they had picked up their snowboards.

Something even stranger happened.

They did not head toward the chairlift. They walked toward the parking lot with their snowboards.

The morning had just started. Why are they quitting already?

I stepped out of my skis. When they got around the corner, I hurried around the other side of the building. I wanted to get to the parking lot from there. That way they would not see me follow them.

I made it to the parking lot just in time to see them get into a van with their snowboards. It was a black van with orange stripes.

Things were getting stranger and stranger. I had seen that van before. It belonged to Budgie McGee, who raced on my ski team.

The van started driving toward me. I stepped back to hide behind the building. It drove past me and out of the parking lot.

I wondered where they were going. I wondered why Budgie was hanging out with a guy who might have put a wire cable up between two trees. I wondered what Cassie was doing with them.

I couldn't think of one good answer that made sense.

I turned around and went back to my skis. I wasn't a very good detective, but I didn't have to waste a great day of skiing.

I lifted my skis and set them on the snow. I stepped into the bindings. I put the ski pole loops around my wrists. I pulled my ski goggles over my eyes.

And I nearly fell backward in surprise.

Sid and Cassie came around the side of the building. They walked toward the ski racks. Budgie must have dropped them off.

Why did they come back?

They didn't have their snowboards with them. So what were they doing back at the ski hill?

I kept watching.

They walked right up to the racks where they had stopped earlier.

Sid leaned over and pulled a snowboard from the rack. Cassie leaned over and picked up another.

It didn't make sense.

Sid slipped his boot into the front snowboard strap. Cassie got ready with her snowboard.

It still didn't make sense. I had seen them take their snowboards into Budgie's van. I had seen them walk back without them. And now they were taking someone else's snowboards.

Both of them pushed off and headed toward the chairlift. Just like they were some of the hundreds of people starting for the day.

Then I knew.

They were on their own snowboards. A yellow one and a red one, almost, but not quite like those they had taken to Budgie's van. That could only mean one thing.

They had stolen those other two snowboards. And Budgie was now driving away with the stolen snowboards.

Eight

I stood in the bright sunshine. The mountainside with its green spruce trees rose beside me. The shouting and laughing of skiers surrounded me. On any other day like this, I would be on the hill skiing, not making my brain hurt by thinking so much.

After a few minutes, I realized something.

Cassie had been the first person to come down the hill after I nearly hit the wire. She knew the snowboarder with the blue hat. She had stolen snowboards with him.

If they were such good friends, maybe it wasn't an accident that she showed up so soon after I fell. Maybe she was looking to see if I had been hurt by the wire.

I smacked my head. It didn't make sense. If she knew about the wire, then why did she run into it herself? If she was part of it, she would have known the wire would be there.

I stood in the sunshine a few more minutes.

I thought of something. A couple of weeks ago, when Garth got hurt, our coach had found him knocked out. Our coach had not seen a wire. So someone must have taken the wire away. That meant that someone had been waiting to untie the wire, probably with pliers, right after Garth fell.

And if that were true for Garth's accident, then someone must have been waiting beside the wire during my run too. That someone was probably Sid. But I ducked in time and then went back up the hill. Sid had to jump on his snowboard and get away instead of untying the wire.

All of this would explain Cassie. If she was part of this, she would think that Sid had pulled the wire down right away. That would explain why the wire surprised her!

I spent a few more minutes in the sunshine thinking about Cassie.

I remembered that I had asked Cassie if she was a tourist here on vacation. I remembered that she had not answered my question. I remembered that she had told me her name instead.

Did that mean she didn't want me to know much about her?

I thought of the way she spoke, like she was from New York. If she was a tourist, she was probably staying at the Big Bear Hotel on the other side of the parking lot.

That gave me an idea.

Nine

I walked toward the front desk at the Big Bear Hotel. My ski boots clunked on the floor. That didn't matter. A lot of people wore their ski boots into the hotel.

I stopped beneath a stuffed moose head that hung above the desk. I looked across the desk at a short guy with red hair and lots of freckles.

"Nathan," I said to him with a big grin. "Do you remember the day I fixed the bindings on your skis?"

"Sure, do," Nathan said. "I still owe you a big favor for that."

"How about now?" I said. "Can you see if someone named Cassie Holt is staying here?"

Nathan frowned. "I could get in big trouble for that. We're not allowed to give out room numbers to anyone."

"I'm not asking for her room number," I said. "I just want to know if she is staying here."

He kept frowning.

"Nathan," I said, "if someone called the hotel and asked to speak with Cassie Holt, what would you do?"

"I would look up her name on the computer and put the call through to her room."

"What if she wasn't staying here?" I asked.

"Then I would tell that person she wasn't at the hotel."

I grinned. "Should I go make that phone call? Or can you tell me right now."

He grinned back. "I'll look it up."

He typed in some letters into his computer keyboard. Then he checked the computer screen.

"Nope," he said. "No Cassie Holt."

"Nuts," I said.

"Hold on," he told me. "There is a John Holt. He has two rooms booked. Do you think one of the rooms is for her?"

"Maybe he is her Dad," I said. "Where are they from?"

"Come on, Keegan," he said. "This information is supposed to be private."

I kept grinning. "Remember how you wouldn't have been able to ski with that cute girl all day? But I fixed your bindings right away, didn't I?"

Nathan looked both directions. He leaned forward and whispered. "They are from Long Island, New York. They got here four days ago, and they will be staying for a week after Christmas."

"Thanks," I said. "Now I owe you."

Nathan looked at something else on the screen. "This is strange," he whispered.

"What?" I said. "What's strange?"

"It says here that the two rooms have been comped."

"Comped?"

"Yes, comped. It means the rooms are free. So are their meals. And their ski tickets. They don't have to pay a thing for their whole visit here."

Nathan looked at me. "That's worth a lot of money," he said. "And I've never seen something like this before. What do you know about this girl?"

"Not enough," I told Nathan. "Not enough."

Ten

I wanted to know more about Cassie Holt. So I went to the ski shop to rent a snowboard.

"You?" the guy behind the counter asked. The guy's name is Bubba. He knew me because I sometimes teach skiing to people who rent skis from him. He's short and wide and has a beard. "Keegan Bishop? Champion downhill racer? On a snowboard?"

"Sure," I said. "Why not?'

"Are you goofy*?"

"Hey," I said. "You don't have to call me names."

He chuckled. "In snowboarding, if you ride with your left foot forward, you're called a regular*. If you ride with your right foot forward, you're called a goofy."

"I don't know if I'm goofy or not," I said, feeling goofy just saying it.

"Try this," he said. He put a snowboard on the carpet. "The bindings are set up for a goofy."

I put my feet into the bindings. I imagined myself on a ski hill.

"It feels, um, goofy," I said.

"That's why they call it that," he told me. "Most people are regulars."

He pulled out a different snowboard. "Take the three-day rental, Keegan. It saves you money. I'll throw in the boots at no charge. With those straps, you could surf in regular boots if you had to. But it's better to use the right gear. The first day will be weird. But if you rent for three days, you won't quit. Once you get used to it, you'll like it."

"Sure," I said. I paid him for three days.

"Yup," he said. "Before you know it, you'll be riding fakie*, and hitting ollies* and wheelies*."

"Huh? Did you just start speaking French or something?"

"You'll be riding backward, jumping bumps, and riding the tail of your snowboard."

"Thanks," I said. "Maybe instead of learning how to snowboard, I'll just learn how to talk like a snowboarder."

"Just enjoy the surfing out there," he said.

"I will."

"Oh, by the way," he said as I got ready to leave. "Keep a good eye on your snowboard. It's worth four hundred dollars."

"I won't lose it," I said.

"I'm not worried about you losing it," he told me. "I'm worried about it getting stolen."

"Stolen?"

"Yes," he said. "Stolen. It's been real bad this year. Thousands of dollars of ski equipment are being stolen every week here at Big Bear."

He whistled. "I mean, add that up. Even if you sold the stolen equipment for half price, that's a lot of money by the end of the ski season."

I thought of Cassie and Sid walking away with two snowboards. That added up to eight hundred dollars. And it only took them five minutes.

"Boy," I said, "thousands of dollars every week. Isn't it about time somebody did something about it?"

Eleven

I wanted to reach the Pipeline run so I could see Cassie. I guessed she would probably be there with the other snowboarders. I was going to ask her to give me some lessons. I thought that would be a good way to get to know more about her.

To get to the Pipeline, I first needed to ride the chairlift to the top of the mountain.

As I got off the chairlift at the top, I fell. It was the first time I had done that since I was seven years old. It was also the first time I had been on a snowboard.

It did not get easier. I fell down so many times that I wished I had brought a pad to protect my rear.

Little kids on snowboards passed me. Old people on snowboards passed me.

Every time I got up, I wobbled a bit and then fell. At the speed I was going, I wasn't going to reach the Pipeline run until after Christmas.

Then, slowly, I began to catch on. Almost all my life I have skied, so at least I knew a little about edges. As I cut across the side of a hill, I learned to dig the uphill edge of my snowboard into the snow to slow down or stop. I learned to turn by skidding one edge or the other.

I also learned to sink into my turns by bending at the knees. To rise out of my turns I straightened them again. It helped when I kept my arms level with the slope of the hill.

I decided not to go to the Pipeline right away. Instead, I kept practicing on other runs.

I went slowly.

On my skis, I could make it all the way down the hill in less than three minutes.

On the snowboard, a half hour passed before I was halfway down. But it was a fun half hour.

I was much slower on my snowboard than on skis. But I started to carve my turns the way I did when I raced. I leaned over the inside edge of the snowboard and dug it into the snow in a long curve. Then I shifted my weight and leaned on the other edge of the snowboard. This made me turn the other direction.

I was not an expert by the time I reached the bottom of the mountain. Riding a fakie? Nope. I only snowboarded backward by accident. An ollie? Nope. My only jumps happened when I could not avoid big bumps. Wheelies? Nope. I could only dream about getting the nose of my snowboard in the air and riding the back half like a surfboard.

Still, I felt okay. I felt like I wouldn't make a fool of myself by the time I rode the chairlift up again and got to the Pipeline.

And I was right.

I didn't make a fool of myself.

Sid did it for me.

Twelve

I saw Cassie's purple ski suit and blond hair right away. She was standing with Sid at the top of the Pipeline. He was wearing his blue knitted hat. They were looking down the hill, away from me.

There was a slight wind. It blew uphill in my face as I snowboarded down toward them. I was snowboarding slowly and carefully, so I wasn't making much noise. Also, the wind must have kept them from hearing what little noise I did make.

They were talking as I got closer. The wind brought their voices right up to me.

"I'm supposed to have dinner with my Dad first," Cassie said to Sid. "Then I can sneak out of the hotel."

"Just don't forget," he told her. "They want to meet you at nine o'clock."

"Hi, guys," I said. I pretended I had not heard what they had said. I pointed at the snowboard strapped to my boots. "What do you think?"

"Keegan!" Cassie grinned, like she was happy to see me. "You're on a snowboard!"

"It's kind of fun," I said. "I was hoping you might give me some lessons."

"Sure," she said.

"No," Sid said. "Leave us alone."

Sid gave me a dirty look. Then he pushed me. I went sliding straight down the hill, almost at full speed.

And straight in front of me was a little girl on skis!

Thirteen

The girl was snowplowing down the hill very slowly. Her little legs were wide apart as she did her best not to fall. She was wearing a cute yellow hat, and she hardly came up to my knees.

If I hit her, it might break every bone in her body.

If I had been on skis, I could have side-stepped her easily.

But I was on a snowboard.

I didn't think I could turn in time. I was afraid if I tried to turn too fast, the snowboard would slide out from under me. If that happened, I would slide into her feet-first. The snowboard would wipe her out.

I was shooting straight toward her. I couldn't fall. I couldn't turn. I felt like a rocket aimed at her back.

There was only one thing to do. I had to time this just right.

I aimed the tip of my snowboard between her skis.

I brought my hands down and grabbed her waist. Instead of crashing into her back, I lifted her and her skis off the ground!

It worked. She was in my arms and traveling at my speed. Her skis were on either side of my waist.

"Wheeeee!" she screamed. "Daddy, this is fun!"

It wasn't fun for me. I still had to get us stopped. Slowly, very slowly, I turned my snowboard and dug the hillside edge into the snow. Slowly, very slowly, we began to stop.

"Wheeee!" she said again. "I like this, Daddy!"

When we were finally stopped, I set her down.

She turned around and looked at me. Her little jaw dropped in surprise.

"You're not my daddy!" she screamed. She began to cry.

Sid and Cassie snowboarded up to us.

Cassie put her arm around the little girl's shoulders. "We'll find your daddy," Cassie said.

The girl stopped crying.

A man higher up on the hill shouted down to us.

"See," Cassie said, "your daddy is coming right now."

Sid looked at me. "Don't think you're a hero. If you don't stop hanging around, you're going to get hurt. Real bad."

"Oh yeah?" I said. It was all I could think of. I felt like a kid on a playground.

"Yeah," he said. "Just like your buddies Garth and Budgie."

"Budgie?" I said. "He's hurt too?"

Sid smiled. "Didn't you hear? He got his van into a little accident. That's what happens to people who mess with us."

Fourteen

Instead of going home that afternoon, I let my parents know I would be staying at the Big Bear ski hill. Although I'm old enough to drive my own car, they like it when I let them know where I am. It saves them from worrying. I figure if my parents are happy, my life is easier.

When I got hungry, I ate a few greasy burgers. When I got bored, I read some ski magazines.

I did what I needed to do to kill time. Cassie was supposed to be meeting somebody. If I could find out who, maybe then I would know why. Why had Garth and Budgie been hurt? How was Cassie involved? Why was all of this happening?

I was going to follow her when she left the Big Bear Hotel. I hung out in the hotel lobby because I wanted to stay warm as long as possible. At night, the mountain air gets very cold.

At a quarter to nine, I went outside and stepped into the shadow of some trees. From there, I could watch the doors of the hotel without anyone seeing me.

Just before nine o'clock, Cassie hurried out of the hotel. She was easy to follow because she didn't look behind her. I was able to stay in deep shadows most of the way.

She surprised me. She went straight toward the chairlift on the side of the mountain.

I kept following.

The chairlift was quiet. It was easy to see, though. There was a bright moon, and the light bounced off the snow. The trees and the chairlift were dark. The snow was gray. It seemed like I was walking through a black-and-white movie.

Two men were waiting for her at the chairlift. I saw that they were on skis.

Skiing? At night? What was going on?

There were lots of trees at the bottom of the hill. I was able to get even closer without being seen. What I saw, though, I didn't like.

One of the men pulled out a pistol and pointed it at her head!

"What is going on?" she said. Her voice reached me clearly across the cold mountain air.

"What is going on?" the man said. It wasn't Sid. I had never heard his voice before. "You're going for a little ride."

The other man stepped out of his skis. He picked up something that had been leaning against a tree.

"Hold this snowboard," he told her.

Then he went inside the chairlift building. A little later, the giant motors started. The chairs on the chairlift began to move.

The man came back outside. He got his skis on again. He sidestepped close to Cassie.

The motors of the chairlift hummed loudly. I could not hear what he said.

I saw him point though. He pointed at the chairlift.

The three of them moved toward a chair. They got on. The chair took them up the mountain. Cassie and two men on skis. One of them still pointed a pistol at her head.

What could I do?

By the time I got the police or any other help, it might be too late.

I waited until they were partway up the mountain. Then I ran toward the chairlift. I got on one of the chairs.

I was afraid if they looked back, they would see me. So I stretched out across the chair. I hoped I would be lost in the shadows.

The chairlift carried me up the mountain behind them.

Fifteen

Although I was in the shadows of the chair, I could see Cassie and the men in the moonlight. They were at least twelve chairs ahead of me. The chairlift took us higher and higher.

I knew this was crazy.

What could I do against two men with a gun?

I told myself maybe I should have gone for help. The way it was now, nobody knew Cassie was in danger. If something went wrong, instead of just Cassie, we would both be in big trouble.

It was too late to change my mind. The only way to get off this chairlift was to wait until it reached the top.

I thought of something else. The two men had skis. Cassie had the snowboard they had given her. How could I keep up? Walking through mountain snow is not easy. If the snow is not packed by skiers, you sink up to your waist. Or deeper.

Then I remembered. At the top of the chair-lift, there is a ski patrol sled. It is always kept there for emergencies. If someone gets hurt, a member of the ski patrol uses the sled to carry the hurt person down the hill.

Could I use the sled to follow these three?

I decided I could. I would lie on it and drag my feet to steer it. As long as I stayed far enough behind them, it might work.

I sure hoped so.

Because a few minutes later, we reached the top of the mountain.

My planning, though, went to waste. When I got off the chair, the man with the pistol was waiting for me.

Sixteen

Y ou think we couldn't see you on the chair-lift, kid?" the man asked. "Now tell us. What are you doing?"

I looked at the other man who was holding Cassie by the wrist.

"Are you all right?" I asked Cassie.

"I get it," the first man said. "Puppy love."

"Let him go," Cassie said. "Keegan doesn't know anything about this."

"Keegan?" the man said. "Keegan Bishop? The racer?"

He laughed. "I'm Fred. My buddy over there is Matt. We're pleased to meet you. And just to make this fair, I'll fill you in on what's going on. That way you don't have to think you died for nothing."

Died? Did he just say died? As in dead?

Fred laughed again. "See, kid. It's about money. Lots of money. Your racing buddies, Garth and Budgie, they liked money too. All they had to do every day here at Big Bear was steal a couple sets of skis. They always made sure they were taking equipment that looked like their own. If they got caught, all they had to do was pretend they grabbed the wrong equipment."

I remembered how Sid and Cassie had walked away with snowboards. "You also had some snowboarders doing the same thing," I said.

"Smart kid. As long as they always took snowboards that looked like theirs, nothing could go wrong. These guys were each making a couple hundred dollars a day, just for walking into the parking lot with the wrong equipment."

"So why are Garth and Budgie in the hospital?" I asked.

"Simple," Fred told me. "They got greedy. It works like this: They steal the equipment. They give it to us. We find buyers. We give them half of what we make. Except Garth and Budgie wanted to go into business on their own. We didn't like that. Our snowboarding buddy set up a cable for Garth to hit. Today, we did a little trick with the tires on Budgie's van. They both learned their lessons."

"There's one thing I don't understand," I said. The longer I kept them talking, the longer Cassie and I could live. Maybe I'd think of something in the meantime. "Why did Sid set up a cable for me? I'm not part of this."

"Budgie switched jersey numbers with you, remember?" Fred said. "All you racers look the same with your helmets on. I was watching the starting gate with binoculars. I had a cell phone to call Sid as soon as Budgie left the gate. When I saw Budgie's number, I called Sid. He was waiting to set the wire up. We planned it to work the same way it did with Garth. As soon as Budgie hit the wire, Sid would take it down again and leave on his snowboard. Of course, you were wearing Budgie's number. So we had to wait to get Budgie on a different day."

"And Cassie?" I asked. "Did she get greedy too?"

Before Fred could answer, Matt, the other guy, finally spoke. "Come on, Fred, we don't have all night."

"What are you going to do?" I asked.

"Cassie is going to have a snowboarding accident," Fred said. "We'll break her leg and leave her on the mountain. We ski out. She stays behind. By morning, she'll be a stiff stiff. Get it kid? A stiff who is stiff from the cold."

I didn't feel like laughing.

"Hey Matt," Fred said, "what should we do with Joe Detective here?"

Matt didn't have a chance to answer.

"Keegan!" Cassie shouted. "Go while you can!" She tossed the snowboard just ahead of me. It landed flat and started sliding downhill away from me.

I dove onto it. Belly first. The bindings hit my stomach hard. But I didn't care. I was on my way down the hill.

I heard a loud snap of gunfire. Snow kicked into my face.

I spun the snowboard to the right. It tilted and nearly threw me into the snow.

Another loud snap. Two more. No bullets hit me.

The hill was so steep already I was at full speed.

If I didn't slow down, the snowboard would kill me instead of the bullets.

I remembered what I had planned to do with the sled. I dug my toes into the ground.

It slowed me some.

By then I was so far away from Fred and his gun that he couldn't hit me.

I slowed some more, enough that I could turn the snowboard and bring it to a stop.

Then I remembered something else. Even though I was halfway down the run, I still wasn't safe. Fred was on skis!

I looked back.

He was a dark shadow against the moonlight and snow. And he was already moving toward me.

I stood as fast as I could. I stepped into the bindings on the snowboard. I strapped them tight around my boots. I started down the hill.

Fred was on skis. I was on a snowboard. And I was in for the run of my life!

Seventeen

I knew if I fell, I was dead. He would catch me before I could get to my feet again.

I had over half a mile of ski run before I reached the bottom and help. He was faster on skis than I could be on my snowboard. The only snowboarding I had done was in the afternoon. And he had a gun. I didn't like any of that.

The good news was that I knew nearly every bump and dip on this ski hill. He would have to go slower in the moonlight than in daylight. I would not have to worry as much.

The other good news was that Cassie was safe from his gun. If I could make it to the bottom alive, they wouldn't dare kill her. I knew their faces and could tell people her death was murder, not an "accident" as they had planned.

I turned hard into a corner.

Ahead of me, the ski hill broke into two runs. One was called the Hammer, because it hit you hard with moguls*. I didn't want to hit moguls. They are like tiny hills. You have to ski around them. Not through them or over them. I can handle moguls at high speeds on skis. But not on a snowboard.

I took the other run. The Monster. It was steeper, but smoother. I picked a straight line and crouched.

The wind tore at my hair and face.

I caught a small bump. I was going so fast it threw me into the air. I concentrated on keeping my knees bent. I concentrated on keeping the snowboard pointed down the hill.

Whomp!

I landed hard. It tilted me to one side. My hand banged the ground. I pushed off and kept on my feet.

I didn't dare look back to see if he was close.

Something touched my sleeve. Like a little kid had tugged on it. It was a bullet. It passed through my jacket and missed my arm. I hadn't heard the noise of the shot because the wind was in my ears.

Was I scared?

So scared I could hardly think. And I still had a quarter mile to go.

I cut to one side. Then the other. I made sure I zigged and zagged so he couldn't guess where I was going.

As I made a turn, I saw him over my shoulder. He was close. So close there wasn't room to park a bus between us. No wonder he had nearly hit me with a bullet!

I knew I didn't have enough room to outrun him.

I did know there was a trail through the trees. It came out near the bottom.

I cut hard. I almost skidded and wiped out.

The black outlines of the trees were coming at me fast. I turned a bit more and hit the trail among the trees.

If I fell now, I didn't need to worry about bullets. Slamming into the trees on either side of the trail would do more damage than a dozen bullets.

I ducked. I bobbed. I fought to keep my balance on the snowboard. Somehow I managed to stay on my feet. Then I shot through a gap in the trees out into the open of another run.

I was nearly at the bottom of the hill!

The parking lot, I told myself, there would be people in the parking lot. If I could get there, I would be safe.

I rounded the final corner of the run. And I saw something at the building that I never expected to see in a million years.

Two police cars. With flashing blue and red lights!

"Hey!" I shouted. "Over here!"

I waved my arms to get their attention.

"Over here!"

I kept shouting and waving. Then I hit another bump.

Because I was standing nearly straight up, and because my arms were too high in the air, I lost my balance.

The snowboard threw me high in the air. I did a half flip. My feet were higher than my head. Coming down felt like slow motion.

I tried to get my hands out to block my fall.

It didn't work.

My head banged into the hard-packed snow. My body crashed down on top of it. And everything went as black as a cave.

Eighteen

I woke up on a couch in the lobby of the Big Bear Hotel.

The first thing I saw was the stuffed moose head above the front desk. I had seen it many times before. This was the first time I felt sorry for it. My head hurt as bad as if someone had cut it off my body and stuffed it too.

"Are you all right, son?" a man asked. He stood above me.

I blinked my eyes. I did not know him.

"My name is John Holt," he said. "I'm Cassie's father."

I tried to sit up. "She's... on... the... mountain!"

It hurt to talk. But I had to tell him. "They... want... to... break... her... leg!"

"Relax, son," he said. "She's right here."

He stepped away.

Cassie stepped up to the couch. Still in her purple ski suit. Still beautiful.

Behind her were police and other people. They were talking to each other and were not looking at us. John Holt went over to join them. That left me and Cassie alone.

"I hope you're okay," she said. "The doctor said you have a mild concussion. He couldn't find any broken bones."

I would hate to know what I'd have felt like if the concussion weren't mild.

"I'm all right," I said. I managed to sit up. "How did you get down from the mountain?"

"Easy," she said. "My dad."

"I don't get it. How did he know?"

Cassie smiled. I liked her smile. I thought it would be good to get her to smile as much as I could.

"How did he know?" she said. "I told him."

"But—"

"It's simple," she told me. "My dad was hired by the Big Bear Ski Resort. He used to be a cop for the New York City police. He retired and became a private detective."

"Big Bear Ski Resort needed a detective?"

"Yes," she said. "The manager was concerned about how much equipment was being stolen. He knew it couldn't be people who just took the snowboards and skis to use themselves. Too much was stolen for that to be true. He thought it might be something more. He even thought it might be Sid and Garth and Budgie. But the manager wanted to know who they were stealing the equipment for. So he hired my dad to look into it."

"That's why your rooms and meals and ski tickets were free!"

"You knew about that?" she asked.

"Um, yes. I asked a friend. I thought you were one of the thieves. I saw you and Sid steal snowboards and put them in Budgie's van. I wanted to know more about you."

"I was trying to help my dad," she said. "He didn't know it, but I decided to make friends with Sid and Budgie. That's why I was following you down the hill the first time we met. I thought you were Budgie because you were wearing his number. Then, when you called me a detective, I freaked out. I thought you were part of it and knew why I had followed."

"That makes sense," I said. "Only you didn't know about the wire trick."

"No," she said. "I didn't know they were trying to get Budgie like they got Garth."

"The meeting tonight?" I asked.

"Dad knew about that. I told him I had found a way to meet the guys who bought the stolen equipment. Dad was angry that I had put myself in danger. He finally let me go to the meeting, but only because he was going to follow and arrest the guys. All I needed to do was talk to them."

"Talk?" I asked. Her dad must have been following me as I followed them. Did I feel silly or what?

"I had a tape recorder in my ski suit," she said. "All I needed was for them to say enough to prove them guilty. Except they had done some checking on me before I got there. They knew my dad was a private detective."

"Which got you in trouble."

"Yes," she said. "The chairlift got me in more trouble. When I went up the lift with Matt and Fred, Dad had to run to get some skis. That's why it took him so long to get to the top. But I didn't know that. All I knew was that he was late. I was afraid they would shoot you before Dad got there, so I threw the snowboard for you."

"I'm glad it worked," I said. "Very, very glad."

"Me too." She surprised me. She leaned forward and kissed my cheek. "You really are a sweetheart."

I didn't know what to say.

"Fred and Matt have been arrested," she told me with a smile. "That means my dad and I still have nearly ten days of vacation left."

"I hope you enjoy it," I said. I wondered if I could continue to run into her on the hill.

"You dummy," she said. "Can't you get anything right?"

"Huh?"

"I just told you I have ten days of vacation left. Maybe you could give me ski lessons. Or maybe I could give you snowboard lessons."

She smiled and gave me another kiss on the cheek. "Ten days can be a lot of time, don't you think?"

come into the cool